Alexandra

QUEEN ALEXANDRA'S CHRISTMAS GIFT BOOK

PHOTOGRAPHS FROM MY CAMERA

To be Sold for Charity

PUBLISHED BY
"THE DAILY TELEGRAPH"
LONDON
1908

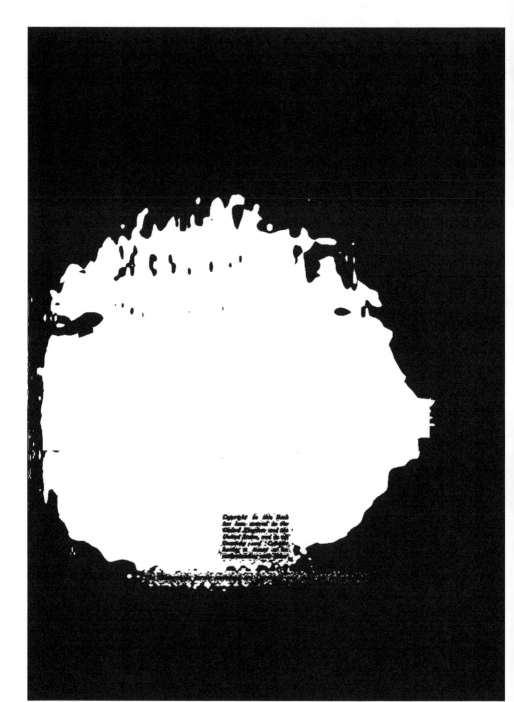

The thanks of the Publishers of this book, issued on behalf of the Queen's charities, are due to:—

The ANGLO ENGRAVING CO., LTD., Photo–Engravers ; MESSRS. R. CLAY & SONS, LTD., MESSRS. CASSELL & CO., LTD., MESSRS. BALLANTYNE, HANSON & CO., LTD., *and* THE LONDON & COUNTY PRINTING WORKS, Printers ; MESSRS. VENABLES, TYLER & CO., LTD., *and* MESSRS. CANNON & CLAPPERTON, LTD., Paper-makers ; MESSRS. F. GRUNEISEN & CO., Bookbinders ; MESSRS. W. & D. DOWNEY, Photographers (for the Frontispiece) ; MR. D. L. HONEYMAN, C.A., of MESSRS. LEVER, ANYON & SPENCE, Chartered Accountants ; *the following Shipping Lines for generously granting facilities for free freightage and the selling of the book on board their steamers*: ABERDEEN (South Africa) ; ALLAN ; AMERICAN ; ANCHOR ; ATLANTIC TRANSPORT ; BOOTH ; CANADIAN PACIFIC ; CUNARD ; DOMINION ; EGYPTIAN ; LEYLAND ; LUND'S BLUE ANCHOR ; NATAL ; NEW ZEALAND ; NIPPON YUSEN KAISHA ; NORD-DEUTSCHER-LLOYD ; P. & O. ; ORIENT-ROYAL ; ROYAL MAIL ; UNION-CASTLE ; WHITE STAR ; *and* WILSON ; *and for kindly assisting the distribution of the book by issuing it in their respective districts*—

The "GLASGOW HERALD," Glasgow ;

The "LIVERPOOL DAILY POST AND MERCURY," Liverpool ;

The "WESTERN MAIL," Cardiff ;

The "EAST ANGLIAN DAILY TIMES," Ipswich.

and, further, to KODAK LIMITED (*whose Kodaks were used by Her Majesty*), *for placing their extensive system of distribution at the Publishers' disposal.*

The King,
George and his two Sons.

Victoria and Myself.

The King.
George and his two Sons.

Victoria and Myself.

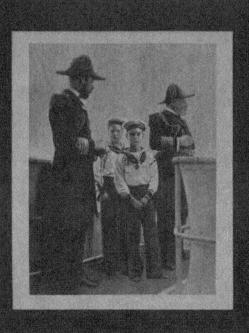

The King,
George and his two Sons.

Victoria and Myself.

The King at Balmoral.

The King, May,
Lady Katherine Coke and Captain Welsh.

George,
Prince of Wales.

Victoria
and Mac.

Party at Balmoral.

Arthur Connaught,
Mr. Hervey and May.

My Two Grandsons wading.

Victoria
and Captain Welsh.

Sir A. Davidson and General Sir D. Probyn.

Fishing Party at Loch Muick.

My Father
and Colonel Kjær—Danish Hussars.

My Father
inspecting a new cavalry repeating rifle.

Testing the new repeating rifle.

Cameron
fishing with me in Scotland.

The Piper Cameron and Victoria.

Duchesse d'Aosta
and Colonel Henry Knollys.

Group at Balmoral.

Shooting Party: Duke of Connaught,
his son, Count de Benckendorff, Sir M. de Bussen,
and Sir C. Hardinge.

Princess of Wales
and Duchesse d'Aosta.

King of Denmark
and his two grandsons.

Victoria
riding at Bernsdorff.

At Bernsdorff.

King of Denmark
and his two grandsons.

Victoria
riding at Bernsdorff.

At Bernsdorff.

Sandringham.

Sandringham.

Wilton House, Salisbury.

Wilton tea-party :
Lord and Lady Lansdowne, Lady de Grey,
and Lord Pembroke.

The Thames—Boulter's Lock.

The Club at Maidenhead.

On the River.

In the Lock.

The King and Emperor
at Reval.

The Mother, Sister, and Children
of the Emperor of Russia.

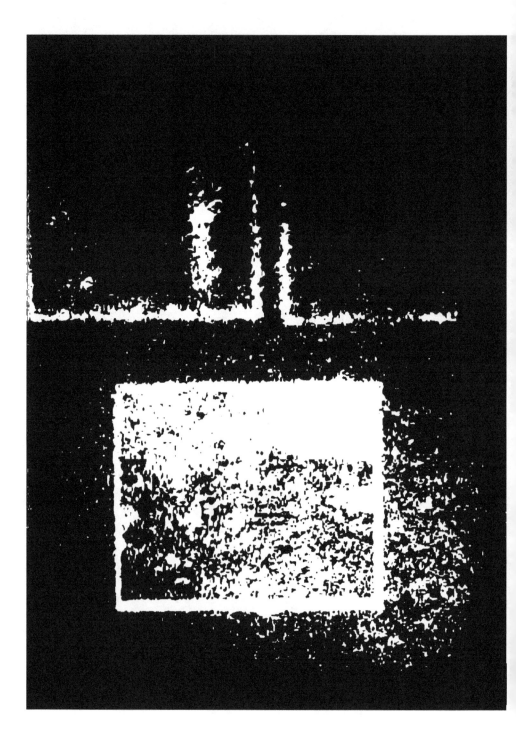

The little Cæsarevitch
with his Sailor Friend.

The Emperor's children and Victoria.

Reval.

On board the Emperor's yacht "Standart."
The young Empress and Victoria.

Sir Charles Hardinge, Sir Arthur Nicolson
and General Sir John French.

Empress of Russia
at Hvidore.

Empress of Russia
and her son Michael
at Hvidore

57

Hvidöre.—Danish Gunboats
during Manœuvres under Prince Waldemar.

Hvidöre.

Copenhagen.—
Group on board.

The Hussars, commanded by Colonel Kjör.
My Father inspecting a new repeating Cavalry Rifle.

Colonel Kjör,
Commander of the Hussars (Danish).

Hussars at Bernsdorff.

King of Greece
in his garden, Athens

Family Group
at Athens.

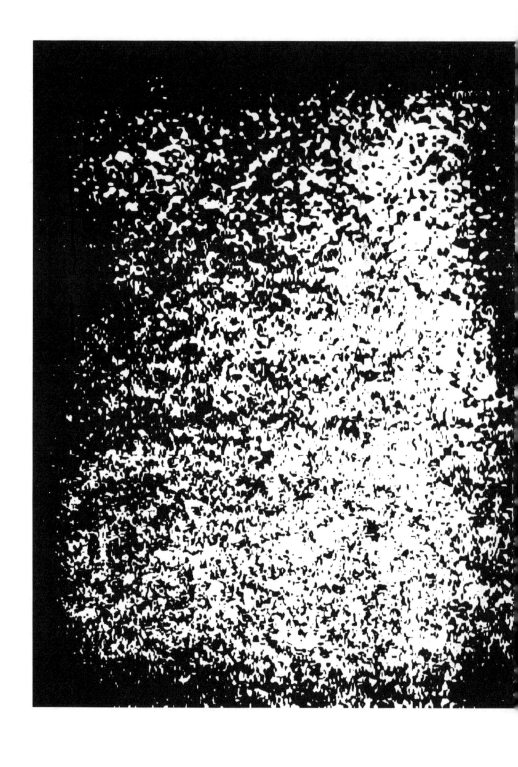

Charles and Maud,
on our way from Vasenkollen.

My Sister the Empress, Victoria,
Maud and Charles (Haakon), Norway.

Charles and little Olav.

The Stadium at Athens
(built of white marble).

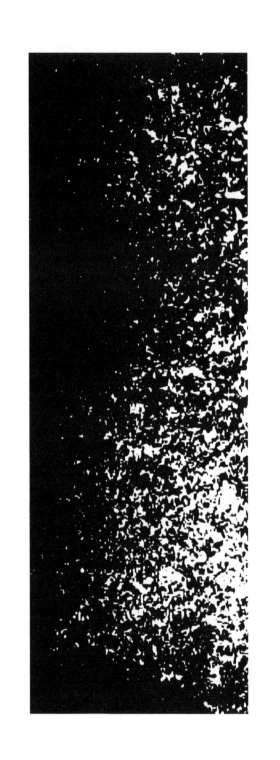

Landing near Christiania for a Picnic.

Fiords—Norway.

Fiords—Norway.

Norway.—The Seven Sisters.

"Victoria and Albert"
at Christiania.

Norway.—The "Polar Star" at Sunset

Professor Tuxen's house.

Victoria
and little Olav.
Mediterranean, 1905.

Miss Knollys and Lady Antrim.
Little Olav.

At Sea—Mediterranean.
Little Olav.

Group on board,
Christiania.

Group on board,
Christiania.

Off Christiania.

Bergen—Norway.

Count de Benckendorff and Lord Errington.

Officers trying to play Diabolo
on board "Victoria and Albert."

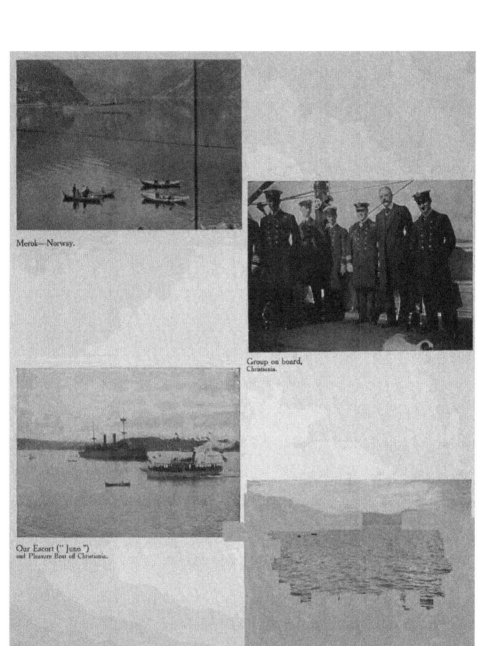

Merok—Norway.

Group on board,
Christiania.

Our Escort (" Juno ")
and Pleasure Boat of Christiania.

Oran—Africa.

My brother George of Greece and
Chevalier Martino, at the Empress of Austria's Villa,
"Achilles," Corfu.

At Corfu.

"The Dying Achilles"
in the Garden of the Empress of Austria's Villa, Corfu.

At Corfu.

The Harbour
at Gibraltar.

Commodore Milne
and Captain V. Stanley.

Ship Boys
on the "Victoria and Albert."

"The Spartan,"
Norway,
1904.

Return of the Prince of Wales from India.
The "Renown" at Corfu.

Our Tea-party at Monrepos, Corfu.

Escort of the Prince of Wales from India.

Merok,
Norway.

At Norway.
Victoria on the swing.

Lord Charles Beresford.

The King
and his Grandson (Little David).

On board our yacht " Britannia."
Our Captain and Crew.

The King inspecting the Fleet
off Cowes, 1907.

Commodore Keppel, Duke of Connaught
and Commodore Crampton.

Edward of Wales
and Sir Charles Cust.

The Lords of the Admiralty.
Naval Review, 1907.

Commodore Keppel & Duke of Connaught on board the King of Greece's Yacht

Men polishing the " Dreadnought "

Commodore Keppel & Duke of Connaught
inspecting the Fleet off Cowes, 1907.

The Fleet saluting the " Dreadnought "
as we pass.

Cowes—Victoria,
Miss Knollys and Lord Knollys.

Commodore B. Milne
and his sub-lieutenant, Pquo.

Victoria,
Colonel Legge and my Dogs.

Commodore Sir B. Milne

Portsmouth.

On leaving Portsmouth.

The Deck of the " Dreadnought."

Submarine A 9.

On the " Dreadnought."

The Raising of the "Gladiator."

The King's Birthday.
The United Bands.

The Opening of the Alexandra Dock,
Cardiff, 1907.

The Pilot,
Norway.

Crew of the " Victoria and Albert,"
Norway, 1904.

Group of Children
taken in Norway.

At Norway.
Sailors of the " Victoria and Albert.'

The Raising of the "Gladiator."

The King's Birthday,
The United Bands.

The Opening of the Alexandra Dock,
Cardiff, 1907.

The House of the Virgin [?]

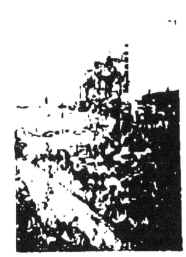

The Raising of the "Gladiator."

The King's Birthday.
The United Bands.

The Opening of the Alexandra Dock,
Cardiff, 1907.

On board "Victoria and Albert."

Opening of the Alexandra Dock,
Cardiff, 1907.

Naval Review
off Portsmouth.

Commodore Sir B. Milne.

" The Nimrod " (Captain Shackleton)
going to the South Pole (1907)

CPSIA information can be obtained
at www.ICGtesting.com
Printed in the USA
BVHW040200301120
594463BV00006B/64